A SECOND LOOK

Dina Anastasio

Senior Authors
Carl B. Smith
Ronald Wardhaugh
Literature Consultant
Rudine Sims

Macmillan Publishing Co., Inc.
New York
Collier Macmillan Publishers
London

Macmillan Publishing Co., Inc.
866 Third Avenue, New York, N.Y. 10022
Collier-Macmillan Canada, Ltd.

Printed in the United States of America 9 R
ISBN 0-02-121710-6

ACKNOWLEDGMENTS

Editor: *Kim Choi*

Art Direction: *Zlata Paces*

Cover Design: *Norman Gorbaty Design Inc.* Illustrators: Diane Patterson, pp. 6-25; James Foote, pp. 26-27; Victoria Beller Smith, pp. 32-33; Terry Fehr, pp. 36-45; Stacey Rogers, pp. 46-52; Victoria Beller Smith, p. 53; Doug Gervasi, pp. 54-63; Victoria Beller Smith, pp. 64-65; Luciana Rosselli, pp. 66-67; Dora Leder, pp. 68-77; Robert Jackson, pp. 80-91; Donald Silverstein, pp. 92-93; Lowren West, pp. 96-123; George Gaadt, pp. 124-125.

The publisher gratefully acknowledges permission to reprint the following copyrighted material:

"Rain Pools" from *I Thought I Heard the City* by Lilian Moore. Copyright © 1969 by Lilian Moore. Used by permission of Atheneum Publishers.

"Old Snake Has Gone To Sleep" reprinted from *Nibble, Nibble* by Margaret Wise Brown. Copyright © 1959 by Margaret Wise Brown. A Young Scott Book by permission of Addison-Wesley Publishing Co.

"I Don't Know Why" from *Whispers and Other Poems* by Myra Cohn Livingston. Copyright © 1958 by Myra Cohn Livingston. Reprinted by permission of Harcourt Brace Jovanovich, Inc.

"Six Foolish Fishermen" from *Six Foolish Fishermen* by Benjamin Elkin. Copyright © 1957 by Childrens Press. Adaptation reprinted by permission of Childrens Press.

"Dick Thompson—The Selfish Boy" from the book *Mrs. Piggle-Wiggle* by Betty MacDonald. Copyright 1947 by Betty MacDonald. Reprinted as adapted by permission of J. B. Lippincott Company.

"What Someone Said When He Was Spanked on the Day Before His Birthday" from the book *You Know Who* by John Ciardi. Copyright © 1964 by John Ciardi. Reprinted by permission of J. B. Lippincott Company.

A Second Look

CONTENTS

The Magic Mirror 6
  A Big Day 12
  Dina Anastasio

Rain Pools 26
  Lilian Moore

Self-Portraits 28
  Dina Anastasio

Old Snake Has Gone to Sleep 34
  Margaret Wise Brown

Images 35
  Joyce Kennedy

Twin Troubles 36
  Allen Yates

I See You ... I See Me 46
  Mirror Writing 53
    Dina Anastasio

The Ghost Catcher 54
    A Tale From India

A Mirror Game 64
    Dina Anastasio

I Don't Know Why 66
    Myra Cohn Livingston

Five in a Pod 68
    Hans Christian Andersen

Word Twins 78
    Joyce Kennedy

The Six Foolish Fishermen 80
    Benjamin Elkin

The Dog and the Bone 92
    Aesop

Fun with Fables 94
    Joyce Kennedy

Dick Thompson—The Selfish Boy 96
  Mrs. Piggle-Wiggle 103
  The Selfishness Cure 114
    Betty MacDonald

**What Someone Said When He Was
Spanked on the Day Before His Birthday** . . 124
    John Ciardi

The Magic Mirror

Dina Anastasio

Mrs. Thomas found the mirror on Friday morning. It was behind a big bed in a shop on John Street, and it didn't take her long to decide to buy it.

"How much?" she asked the storekeeper.

"Ten dollars," he told her.

Mrs. Thomas looked at the mirror. It was very old, and it needed paint badly.

"Ten dollars is a lot for something that old," she said.

"But it's special," said the storekeeper, with a smile on his face.

6

"Special? How is it special?"
asked Mrs. Thomas,
looking very puzzled.

"You'll see, you'll see," said
the storekeeper. Mrs. Thomas waited
for the storekeeper to say something
more. But that was all he said
about the mirror.

Mrs. Thomas was more puzzled
than ever. But there was something
about the mirror that made her want
to buy it. She gave the man
ten dollars, and he helped her
carry it to her car.

FOR SALE

On her way home, Mrs. Thomas
stopped at a store for some red paint.
She worked on the mirror for the rest
of the morning. By two o'clock
in the afternoon the paint was dry.
Mrs. Thomas carried the mirror inside
and put it next to the kitchen table.
Then she stood back and stared at it.
It really was a wonderful mirror.

"I'll bet this mirror is
a hundred years old," Mrs. Thomas said
to herself. And she began to think
of all the people who might have owned
it before her. Painters and storytellers
and maybe even a clown or two.

When Ricky and Pam came home,
Mrs. Thomas was still looking
at the mirror.

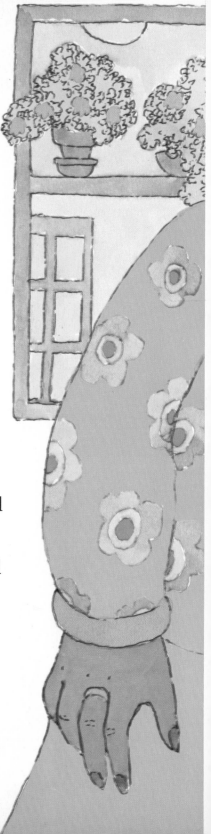

8

"Where did you get **that?**"
Ricky laughed.

"That is the most awful thing
I have ever seen!" said Pam.

"I found it in a little shop,"
Mrs. Thomas told them. "And I think
it's wonderful. And very special."

"**Oh, Mother!**" said Pam and
Ricky, and they went out to play.

9

When Mr. Thomas saw the mirror, he didn't say anything at all. He just stared. Then he went into the living room to read the paper.

But Mrs. Thomas didn't care. She still thought the mirror was wonderful and very special.

Supper that night was **almost** like other nights. Ricky didn't like the beans. Pam didn't like the meat. Mr. Thomas didn't like the milk that fell on the floor. It was **almost** like other nights. The **almost** was the mirror.

Every time someone shouted or cried or made a face, the mirror would show them what they looked like. They would see how awful or silly or impossible they looked, and they would start to laugh.

When Pam said, "I hate this meat!" she happened to look in the mirror. She started to laugh. Pam really does look very funny when she's trying to be mad. She had just never seen herself looking mad before.

By the time supper was over, everyone was happy. Everyone liked everyone else. That night the whole family played cards. And no one screamed or cried or got mad or anything else. It was very, very nice.

A Big Day

The next Friday was to be
a big day for the Thomas family.
Pam was to play a clown
in the school play. Ricky was
to pitch his first baseball game.
Mr. Thomas had to present his
building plan at his office.
And Mrs. Thomas, who had just become
the head of an art school, had
to talk in front of one hundred
very important people.

By Sunday everyone was
nervous. Pam didn't know her lines.
Ricky couldn't get one ball over home plate.
Mr. Thomas wasn't sure what would be
the best way to present his plan. And
Mrs. Thomas couldn't eat, or sleep.
Supper that night was happy again,
because of the mirror. But it was
quieter. No one said very much.
Everyone was thinking about Friday.

That night, after everyone else
had gone to bed, Mrs. Thomas tiptoed
into the kitchen. She turned
on the light and stood in front
of the mirror. She stood as tall
as she could. Then she put her hands
behind her back and smiled
into the mirror. The mirror smiled back.
Mrs. Thomas began to talk. She didn't
talk loudly, for she didn't want
to wake her family. She talked just
loud enough for the woman in the mirror
to hear.

Mrs. Thomas stood before the mirror all night long. She pretended that it was Friday and she was talking to one hundred people. She practiced and practiced. By the time the sun came up, she knew that she would be fine on Friday.

Before she went to bed, she clapped. And the woman in the mirror clapped, too.

"You are magic!" said Mrs. Thomas. She wasn't at all nervous any more.

The next night, when everyone was sound asleep, Mr. Thomas tiptoed out to the kitchen. He turned on the light and stood in front of the mirror. He stood as tall as he could. Then he put his hands behind his back and smiled into the mirror. The mirror smiled back.

Mr. Thomas took out his papers. He pretended that it was Friday at his office. He talked softly, so as not to wake his family. He practiced all night long. When the sun came up, he knew just what he would say on Friday.

"**You are magic!**" he said to the mirror. Mr. Thomas was very happy.

The next night, when her mother and father had gone to bed, Pam tiptoed into the kitchen. She had on her clown hat, but when she looked into the mirror, she was still Pam. Pam didn't want to be Pam that night. She wanted to be a clown—a **real** clown.

She pulled herself way, way up, until she was very tall. She put her hands behind her back and made a funny face. Then she smiled at the mirror. And the mirror smiled back. And this time— it was a **real** clown that smiled out of the mirror. It wasn't Pam at all.

Pam practiced her lines all night long. And when the sun came up, she knew her part very well.

Before she went to bed,
Pam stood before the mirror and clapped.
And the clown clapped back at her.

"**You are magic!**" Pam told
the mirror. She was very happy.

The next night it was Ricky's turn.
When the house was very quiet,
he took out his baseball and bat.
Then he tiptoed into the kitchen
and stood in front of the mirror.
Ricky didn't smile. He just looked grim.
Then he picked up his bat and swung it
behind him. The boy in the mirror
did the same.

Ricky closed his eyes and waited
for the pitcher to throw the ball.

And then he swung.

"**Home run!**" shouted Ricky.

    Ricky practiced his swing
until two in the morning. When he was
sure that it was just right, he put
his bat on the floor. Then he
picked up his baseball. The boy
in the mirror did the same.
Ricky wound up. His arm flew back.
He closed his eyes and started
to pitch the ball.

But he stopped just in time.

"**Strike one!**" shouted Ricky.

Ricky wound up again.
His arm flew back. But again he stopped,
and the ball did not leave his hand.

"**Strike two!**" shouted Ricky.

Ricky wound up once more.
He looked in the mirror, and he saw
a boy. It seemed to Ricky that the boy
was not holding a baseball. He was
holding a bat, and he was waiting
for Ricky to pitch the ball.
Ricky's arm swung back, and

HE THREW THE BALL!

Just as Ricky was about to yell **"Strike three!"** a loud cracking noise sounded throughout the house.
Mr. and Mrs. Thomas ran into the kitchen, with Pam right behind them.
They stared at the mirror. And they all understood just what had happened.
Mr. and Mrs. Thomas didn't say anything. Pam was quiet, too.

Ricky just said, "I got a little carried away."

And then they all went back to bed.

No one talked to anyone else the next day. They were all thinking about Friday. They were all very nervous. They missed the mirror, but no one got mad at Ricky. They all understood what it was like to get carried away.

On Friday morning they met for breakfast.

"I've never been so nervous in my life," said Pam.

"Me, too," everyone said together.

"I can't pitch," Ricky said.

"You did a pretty good job the other night," laughed his father.

"I **was** pretty good, wasn't I?" asked Ricky.

"You were, indeed," said his mother.

"I was **wonderful** in front
of that mirror," said Pam. "I just wish
I could be a clown in front
of the mirror again. That's better
than in front of hundreds of people."

"You're right," said Mr. Thomas.

"Maybe," said Mrs. Thomas, "we can
all pretend that we're in front
of the mirror. Then we'll be as good
as we were before."

23

And that is just what they did!

The mirror was at Ricky's baseball game.

The mirror was at Pam's play.

24

The mirror was at Mr. Thomas's office.

The mirror was at Mrs. Thomas's school.

It smiled.

It clapped.

It looked just like a clown.

And it didn't crack when Ricky threw strike three!

And everyone was very good indeed!

25

RAIN POOLS

The rain
litters
the street
with mirror splinters
silver and
brown.

Now
each piece
glitters with

sky
cloud
tree

upside down.

—Lilian Moore

27

Self-Portraits

Dina Anastasio

A self-portrait is a picture of an artist painted by the artist himself. An artist needs a mirror to draw a self-portrait. On the next few pages you will see what some artists saw when they looked in their mirrors.

Here Norman Rockwell uses a mirror to help him paint a self-portrait. ⟳

This self-portrait was painted in 1498 by Albrecht Dürer when he was 27 years old. ⟳

Vincent Van Gogh painted many self-portraits during his lifetime. This one, painted in 1890, was his last. ◁

This self-portrait, by Leonardo da Vinci, was made about 1510. The artist used red chalk to give a feeling of age to the drawing. ◁

Malvin Gray Johnson painted this self-portrait when he was a young man. In the back we can see one of his other paintings. ▷

Artists sometimes use pictures in place of mirrors. Gwendolyn Smith, age 7½, is using the picture in the corner as a mirror of herself.

Artists have been looking in mirrors and drawing self-portraits for hundreds of years. This is how Everett Kelsey, age 8, drew himself.

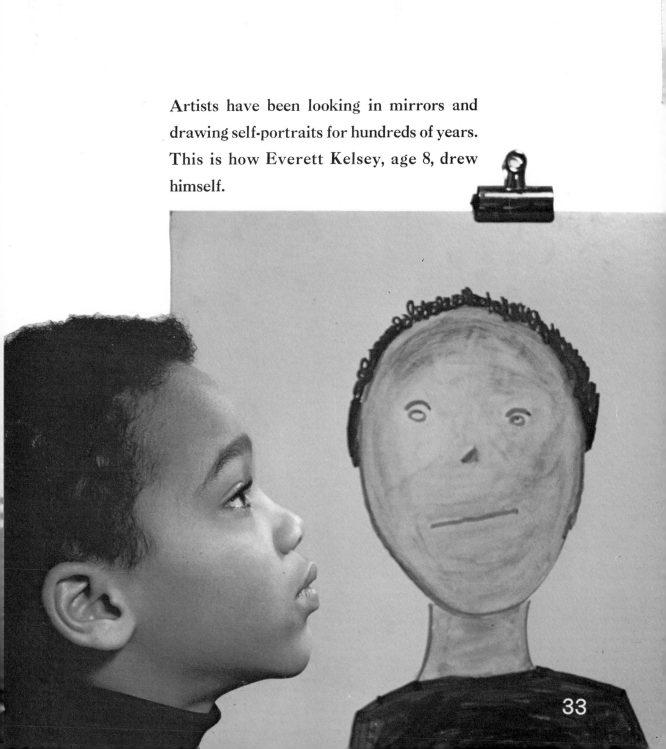

Sun shining bright on the mountain rock
Old snake has gone to sleep.
Wild flowers blooming round the rock
Old snake has gone to sleep.
Bees buzzing near the mountain rock
Old snake has gone to sleep.
Sun shining warm on the mountain rock
Old snake has gone to sleep.

—Margaret Wise Brown

Old Snake Has Gone to Sleep

Images

Sometimes a poem seems to mirror a part of the world. Words can be like mirrors. They can help us to see!

When you look in the mirror, you see your image. A poem has images, too. Old snake is the most important image in this poem. But there are others, too. If you were to make a drawing for this page, what would you put with Old Snake?

The poem not only makes us see, but makes us hear and feel, too. Can you find a sound word? Can you find a touch word?

Twin Troubles

Allen Yates

Have you ever thought what it would be like to have a twin? When I was growing up, I always had a very special friend—my twin brother, who looked just like me.

Our family lived in a log cabin on
a ranch in the West. There were not
many children living near us. So I was
lucky to have a twin brother to play
with. Our cabin was beside a little
stream. There were open fields, and
woods, and a big hill for us to play on.

Every night after school my brother
and I would walk along paths we had
made through the woods, beside the
stream, and up the hill. We named each
special place and kept watch for new
plants, animals, and birds. We watched a
family of rabbits who lived in a rock
pile on top of the hill. A family of
possums who lived in a tree in the
woods became our friends. And every
summer we waited for the deer, crows,
and ducks. They came to our ranch to
care for their babies in the woods
and fields.

My brother and I went to school in a one-room schoolhouse near our ranch. There were only seven other children in the school. We all had the same teacher. The children in each grade sat in their own row of seats. The teacher would spend a little time with the children in each row while the others did their work.

I remember one day when our teacher kept me after school. I had been bad during practice for our second-grade play. My brother had gone out to play in the snow before we walked home. I was very angry because I had to stay late. When the teacher said I could go, I ran out, gave the door a good slam, and started running home to our cabin. I didn't stop to talk to my brother. When the teacher saw me slam the door, she ran out to shout at me. But I was already out of sight. She saw my brother and started shouting at him. My poor brother had a hard time making her understand that he had not done anything wrong.

My brother got me in trouble just as often as I got him in trouble.

Our teacher had a tiny little trailer beside the schoolhouse. She would spend the night in the trailer if there was too much snow to drive back to town. She often went into the trailer during lunch. We all thought she was taking a nap.

One day my brother found a pile of snow beside the trailer that was big and hard. After lunch my brother and some other children climbed up on the pile of snow and peeked in the window. They wanted to see if they could catch our teacher sleeping. She pretended not to see them. But that afternoon each of the "snoopers" had to write "It is not nice to snoop. I will never snoop again," three hundred times on the blackboard.

Because my brother had peeked a
few times, our teacher thought that I
must have done it, too. I didn't even
know what had happened during lunch.
But that afternoon I had to stand
beside my brother and write "It is not
nice to snoop. I will never snoop again,"
three hundred times on the blackboard.

My teacher must have thought that because my brother and I looked so much alike, we were alike inside, too. This wasn't so. But it was a hard thing to make people understand.

One time our teacher took all of us on a field trip to town. We went to a few big stores, a bakery, and a bank. Since we were all country children, we thought these new places were more wonderful than you can ever imagine. Under the bank there was a big room with rows and rows of little boxes. People kept things there that they didn't want to lose. It was like walking inside a safe.

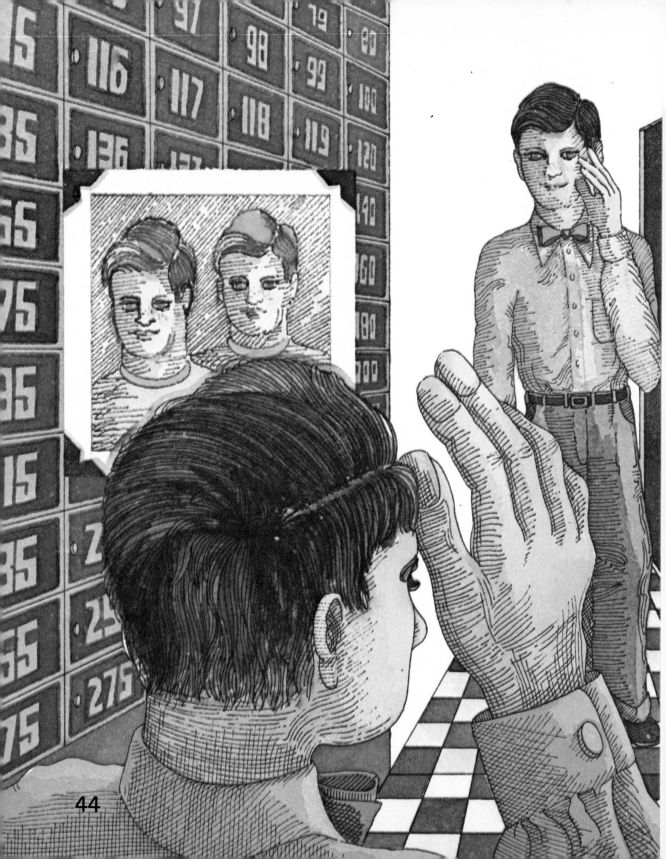

44

I got a little nervous, so I started looking for my brother. I saw him way down at the other end of the room. We started to walk to each other. As he came closer, I began to walk faster. I wanted to talk to him very much. Just as I was about to say his name, I walked into a wall-to-wall mirror and almost fell down. I had never seen such a big mirror before. I really thought my twin brother was walking up to me.

Everyone thought it was very funny that I had walked into the mirror. But I didn't. You have no idea what it's like to come face to face with your brother, and find that it's really you.

These are only a few of the funny things that happened to me because I was a twin. Growing up with a twin brother was a lot of fun. But there were times when it sure was a lot of trouble!

I see you . . . . .

This is a piece of glass.

I can see <u>through</u> this piece of glass.

. . . I see me . . . .
Dina Anastasio

This is glass, too.

I can see <u>me</u> in this piece of glass.

What's the difference?

The difference is on the back of the glass.

48

There isn't anything on the back
of my glass window.

The back of my mirror is painted silver.

Light is going through the window.

The light doesn't go through the mirror. It hits the silver and bounces back.

This is my baby brother. He thinks it's a very nice day.

This is my baby sister. She thinks it's a very nice baby.

51

My window is
still here.

So is my mirror.
But you can't see
the window or the
mirror because the
lights are out and it
is dark outside. There
is no light, so we
can't see very well.

52

Mirror Writing

Hold this
up to a
mirror.

Can you
read what
it says?

I peeked in the
mirror, and
what did I see?
A scary old ghost
was staring at me!

The Ghost Catcher
A Tale from India

Now this is a very old story from India. It is about a young barber who did not really want to be a barber. And it is about a ghost—two ghosts.

The young barber's name was Ved. Ved didn't like being a barber. He didn't like cutting men's hair or shaving their faces. He really wanted to be a farmer.

But Ved's father was a barber. And when Ved's father died, all he left his son was his bag of barber tools— razors, brushes, combs, and a mirror. So what could Ved do? He tried to be a barber, too. In those days, you had to do whatever your father did.

Well, Ved was a clever boy, but he wasn't a good barber. And after a while people stopped coming to him.

"He's not as good a barber as his father," they said.

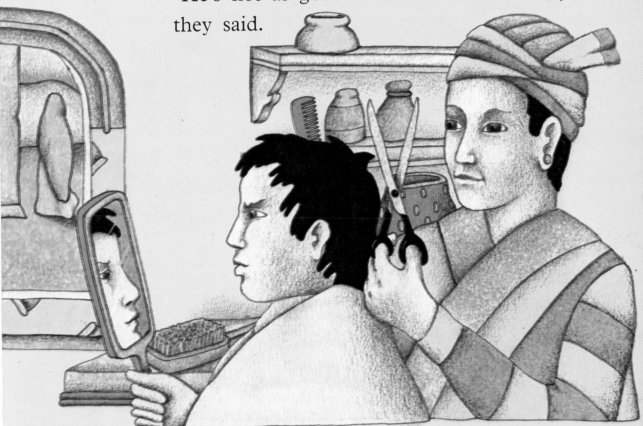

"I'd rather be a farmer," Ved thought. "But if I have to be a barber, I will leave this town. I will go to the city. There no one will know that my father was a better barber than I."

And so Ved picked up his bag of barber tools—razors, brushes, combs, and a mirror. He set off for the city.

Ved walked all morning and he walked all afternoon. When night came, Ved sat under a willow tree to rest. The city was still a long way off. So Ved decided to spend the night under the willow tree. "Then I can start out fresh in the morning," he said to himself. Ved lay down on the ground and fell asleep at once.

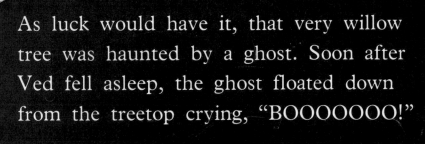

As luck would have it, that very willow tree was haunted by a ghost. Soon after Ved fell asleep, the ghost floated down from the treetop crying, "BOOOOOOO!"

Ved woke up at once. "What a bad dream," he said to himself. "I dreamed this willow tree was haunted by a ghost."

"BOOOOOOO!" cried the ghost again. Now he was right at Ved's ear. This was not a dream! Ved had to think fast.

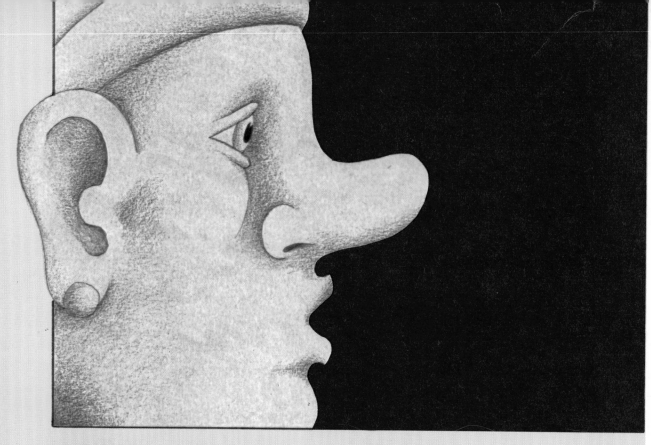

"Don't you come close to me, ghost,"
Ved said quickly. "D-Do you know what
I am? I-I'm a GHOST CATCHER!
That's what I am! I catch ghosts and
put them in my ghost bag."

And with that Ved opened his bag
of barber tools and pulled up the mirror.
"Here, let me show you one ghost
I've caught tonight," he said. Ved held
the mirror up to the ghost's face.
"I think I'll put you in the bag, too."

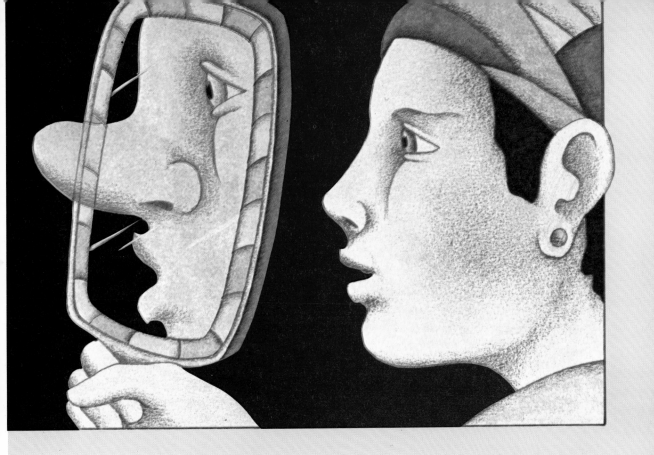

The ghost looked into the mirror—and
what did he see? His own face, of course.
But he didn't know that. He thought
the barber really had caught a ghost
in the bag.

"Oh, please," said the ghost, "don't
put me in your ghost bag. I'll give
you anything you want. Just let me go."

"Anything I want?" said Ved. "Then I
want a bag of gold. Maybe two bags."

Zip! In a second two bags of gold were at Ved's feet.

"Good enough," Ved said. "I won't put you in my bag this time. But remember, if you bother me again, into the ghost bag you go." As soon as Ved let the mirror fall back into the bag, the ghost was gone.

Ved never did go to the city. He took some of the gold the ghost had given him and he bought himself a farm. He bought cows and pigs and horses. Ved was a fine farmer. He didn't have to cut hair or shave faces any more. But Ved kept his bag of tools—and that was very clever of him.

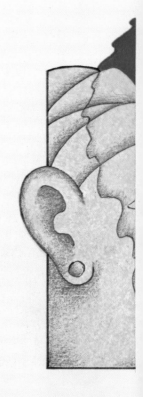

For, as luck would have it, the ghost met his friend one day and told him everything that had happened.

At the end of his story, the friend laughed and laughed.

"Hoo, hoo, hoo," he laughed. "No man can catch a ghost. And there is no such thing as a ghost bag. You have been tricked."

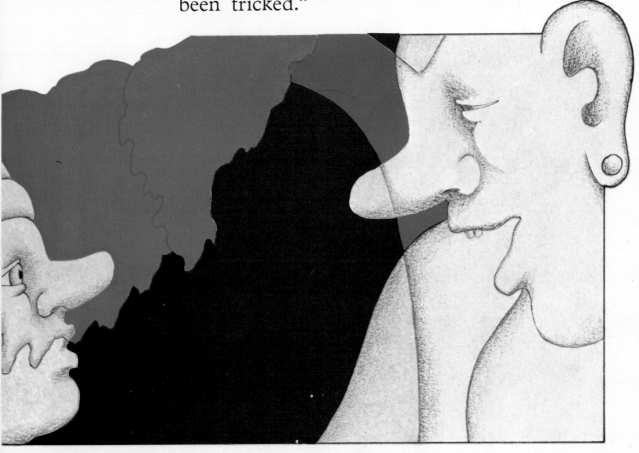

"Well, go and see for yourself,"
the ghost said. "But don't be angry
at me if that man puts you in his bag."

The friend floated over to Ved's house.
He peeked through the window.

Ved was eating his supper. He felt
a cold wind and looked up. Another
ghost! Ved ran to get his bag of tools.
Quickly, he opened the bag and pulled
out the mirror. Then he held the mirror
up on the window and shouted, "Come
on in! I"ll put you in the bag, too!"

The friend took one look at the ghost in the mirror and floated off as fast as he could go.

From that time on, no ghost ever dared to bother Ved again. But Ved was clever enough to keep his bag of barber tools handy. But he never had to use them again.

Mirror Game

Dina Anastasio

This game is played
by two people.

One player is **IT**.
The other player is **ITS**
reflection in a mirror.

The player who
is the reflection
must do
everything **IT**
does—

very
quickly—just
as if he is
ITS real reflection.

I DON'T KNOW WHY

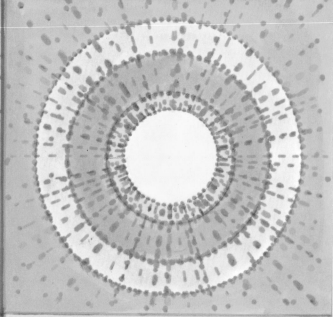

I don't know why
the sky is blue
or why the raindrops
splatter through
or why the grass
is wet with dew...
do you?

I don't know why
the sun is round
or why a seed grows
in the ground

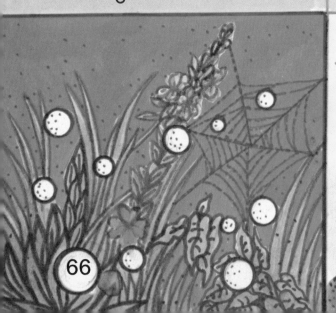

or why the thunder
makes a sound...
do you?
I don't know why
the clouds are white

or why the moon
shines very bright
or why the air
turns black at night...

—Myra Cohn Livingston

Five in a Pod

Hans Christian Andersen

There lived five peas in one pod. The peas were green and the pod was green so they thought the whole world was green. The pod grew and the peas grew. They made themselves as cozy as they could and sat close together in a row. The sun warmed the pod, and the rain made it nice and clean. It was quite cozy, there in the pod. And the peas sat growing bigger and bigger.

At last one pea said, "Are we to sit here forever? We'll all get backaches from too much sitting in one place. I have an idea that something is going on outside. It's just a feeling I have."

Weeks went by. The pod turned yellow and the peas turned yellow. "The whole world is turning yellow," they said. And they had every right to say so.

All at once they felt a pull at the pod. The pod was broken off and held a second in a boy's hand. Then it was pushed into a coat pocket.

"It won't be long now before we're out in the world," said the peas. And they could hardly wait until the time came.

"I wonder which of us will become the most remarkable," said the smallest of the five. "Well, we'll soon find out."

Pop! The pod opened and all five peas came rolling out into the bright sunshine. The boy looked at them. The peas were just what he needed for his peashooter. He put one of the peas into the peashooter and let it go.

"Here I go," cried the pea, "flying out into the wide world! Catch me if you can." And he was gone.

"I," yelled the second, "shall show everyone how far I can go!" And away he went.

The next two were lazy. They said, "We'll get wherever we're going. It won't make any difference *what* we do. So we'll just keep rolling along." But they were not rolling very long. They got into the peashooter just the same.

Soon it was time for the last one. "What will be, will be," said the last as he went flying out of the peashooter. He flew up to an old board under an attic window. He landed in a crack filled with some moss and soft earth. There he lay, alone, and hidden by the moss—forgotten by all.

"What will be, will be," he said.

In the attic lived a poor woman and her little daughter. The mother went out to work every day. She did all kinds of hard work. But she was still as poor as ever.

At home in the attic was her only child, the little daughter, who had been sick for a whole year. She showed no signs of getting better. Sadly the mother thought her child would never get well. All day long the sick girl lay in her bed quietly, while her mother was away at work.

One spring morning the mother was about to leave for work. Just then the sun came through the window. The sick child turned her eyes to the window.

"Mother, there's a little green thing looking in at the window," she said. "See, it's moving in the wind. What can it be?"

The mother went to the window and opened it a little. "Why, it's a tiny plant," she said. "A pea plant. It's taken root and has pushed up its green leaves. How did it ever find its way here? There, now you have something pretty to look at."

She moved the child's bed nearer to the window. Then she went off to work.

Later that day when the mother came back, the little girl looked very happy. "Mother, I believe I'm going to get well," she said. "All day long the sun has been shining on the little plant. It's coming along fine—and so am I. I know I'll be able to get up soon. It would be so nice to go out into the sunshine again."

"That would be so wonderful!" said the mother. But she really did not believe such a thing could happen. Still, she was thankful to the little plant that had made her sick child so happy. So she took a little stick and put it up right next to the plant. Then she tied a piece of string from the window sill to the upper part of the window. Now the little pea had somewhere to climb.

"Oh, look," cried the mother one morning, "our little plant has a flower!" And now she dared hope that her sick child would get well at last.

75

About a week later, the child was able to get up for the first time. She sat for a whole hour in the warm sunshine. The window was wide open. And there outside stood a pea flower in full bloom. The little girl leaned over and softly kissed the flower.

"This is a day of great joy," said the happy mother. And she smiled at the pea plant as if to say *thank you.*

Well, and now—what about the other peas? The first one, who went flying out into the wide world crying, "Catch me if you can!" landed on a rooftop. Soon a bird caught him and ate him up. The lazy two met with another bird, who made short work of them also. The one who was going to show everyone how far he could go ended up in a garbage can. He lay there in the water getting bigger and bigger. "How big and round I'm getting," he said. "In no time I will be the fattest and roundest pea around. I believe I'm the most remarkable of the five out of our pod."

But at the attic window stood the little girl, her eyes bright and shining. She was looking at the pretty pea plant. Its fresh green shoots were beginning to climb all over her window.

Word Twins

Do you know that some words are twins? They sound alike and some of them are spelled alike, but they don't mean the same thing. Just like people, they are not alike in every way.

Reflection is such a word. It can mean an image in a mirror or water, but it can also mean careful thinking.

Look at these words. Can you think of two meanings for each?

bat	bank	ball	can
pitcher	sock	lap	rock
second	trunk	park	pitch
trip	band	land	

Bark (tree)

Bark (dog)

78

Some word twins are not spelled
alike. They sound alike, though!

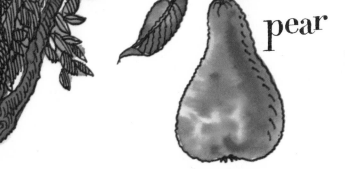

pear

pair

Here are more word twins.
Can you tell the meanings of these words?

I	eye
beat	beet
bear	bare
deer	dear
hear	here

You could put word twins together in a sentence:

I ate eight cookies!

You can start a word twin book if
you wish. Decorate the cover with
some word twin illustrations. Then
when you find more word twins,
write them in your book!

79

This is a play about a girl and six foolish brothers who are fishermen. Because the fishermen are men, it does not mean that only boys can play their parts. Long ago, men played the parts of women in all plays. And women often played the parts of men. The parts in *Six Foolish Fishermen* may be played by either boys or girls.

The Players

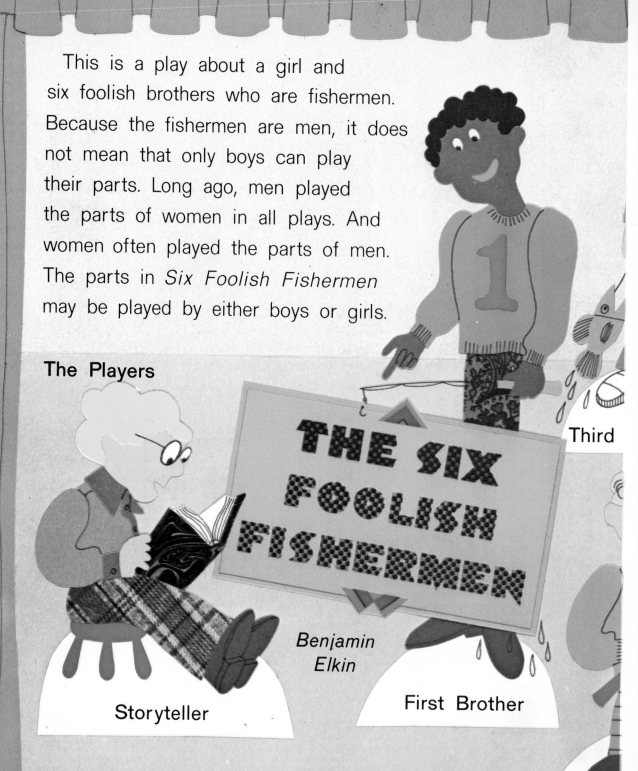

THE SIX FOOLISH FISHERMEN

Benjamin Elkin

Storyteller

First Brother

Third

Second

80

Brother

Sixth Brother

Fifth Brother

Fourth Brother

Brother

Girl

81

Storyteller: Once there were six brothers who decided to go fishing. So they went to the river and picked good spots to rest and fish.

First Brother: I will sit in this boat.

Second Brother: And I will kneel on this raft.

Third Brother: And I will lean on this log.

Fourth Brother: And I will stand on this bridge.

Fifth Brother: And I will lie on this rock.

Sixth Brother: And I will walk on this bank.

Storyteller: And that is just what they did. Each brother fished from the spot he had picked. And each one had good luck. But when it was time to go home, the brothers became a little nervous.

First Brother: We have been near the river, and over the river, and on the river. Maybe one of us fell into the river and was drowned. I shall count all the brothers to be sure there are six of us.

Storyteller: And he began to count.

First Brother: *(counting his brothers)*
I see one brother on the raft.
That's **one.**
And another on the log.
That's **two.**
And another on the bridge.
That's **three.**
And another on the rock.
That's **four.**
And another on the bank.
That's **five.**
Only **five!**
Oh, dear me!
We have lost a brother!

Second Brother: Can it really be?
Has one of us been drowned?
And have we really lost a brother?

Storyteller: And he, too, began to count.

Second Brother: I see one brother on the log.
That's **one.**
And another on the bridge.
That's **two.**
And another on the rock.
That's **three.**
And another on the bank.
That's **four.**
And another in the boat.
That's **five.**
Only **five!**
What will our dear mother say?

Third Brother: Let me count!

I see one brother on the bridge.

That's **one.**

And another on the rock.

That's **two.**

And another on the bank.

That's **three.**

And another in the boat.

That's **four.**

And another on the raft.

That's **five.**

Five in all! Oh, unhappy day!

Why did we ever come here for one of us

to be drowned!

Storyteller: Then the fourth brother counted,

and the fifth and the sixth.

(The brothers run around counting.)

Storyteller: Each one counted only five brothers. All the brothers went back to the river and ran sadly up and down the side of the river, trying to see if they could see their poor drowned brother in the water. Then along came a girl. The girl had been fishing, too. But she had not been able to catch any fish at all.

Girl: What's the matter? You have a lot of fish. Why do you all look so sad?

Fourth Brother: Because six of us came here to fish, and now there are only five of us left. One of our dear brothers has been drowned!

Girl: What do you mean, only five left? How did you get that?

Fifth Brother: Look, I'll show you.
(points to his brothers)
One...Two...Three...Four...Five...
Six of us came here and now only five are going back. Sad is the day!

Storyteller: The girl turned to hide her smile, and then she turned back.

Girl: I think I can help you find your lost brother. When I squeeze your hand, I want you to count.

Storyteller: As hard as she could, she squeezed the hand of each of the brothers in turn.

First Brother: *(yelling as Girl squeezes his hand)*
ONE!

Second Brother: *(crying and jumping up and down because of the hard squeeze)* TWO!

Third Brother: THREE!

Fourth Brother: FOUR!

Fifth Brother: FIVE!

Sixth Brother: SIX!

Storyteller: SIX! The brothers looked at each other in surprise. There were six of them again! They jumped for joy and hit each other on the back. And they turned to the girl.

Sixth Brother: Here, take all our fish. We can never thank you enough for finding our dear lost brother.

Storyteller: So the girl took the fish. And the six foolish fishermen went home.

THE DOG AND THE BONE

Aesop

One day a dog, carrying a bone in his mouth, was walking over a big river.

Looking down from the bridge, he saw his own reflection in the water. But he thought it was another dog.

He began to bark, for he was greedy for the other's bone. As soon as he opened his mouth, his own bone fell into the water. And it was lost forever.

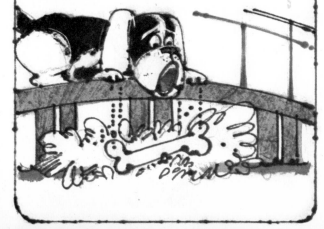

A Thought:

It is better to take care
of your own things
than to be greedy
for those of others.

Fun With Fables

What To Do

The story you read called "The Dog and the Bone" is a fable. A fable is a very short story. Fables are nearly always about animals, but they teach something that people can learn. If you liked Aesop's fable about the dog and the bone, and if you like puppets, here is something for you to do.

First, go to the library and get a book of Aesop's fables. Then read the fables with a friend. Pick out one that you both like. Now make some animal puppets. Make the animals that are in the fable you picked.

Bone

Ant

Paper makes
finger puppets.

Grasshopper

A mitten
makes a dog.

Together with your friend, plan a play about the fable. Use your puppets to play the parts. You and your friend move the puppets and say the words.
If there is only one animal in the story, one of you can be the storyteller.
Now do your play for your class and teacher!

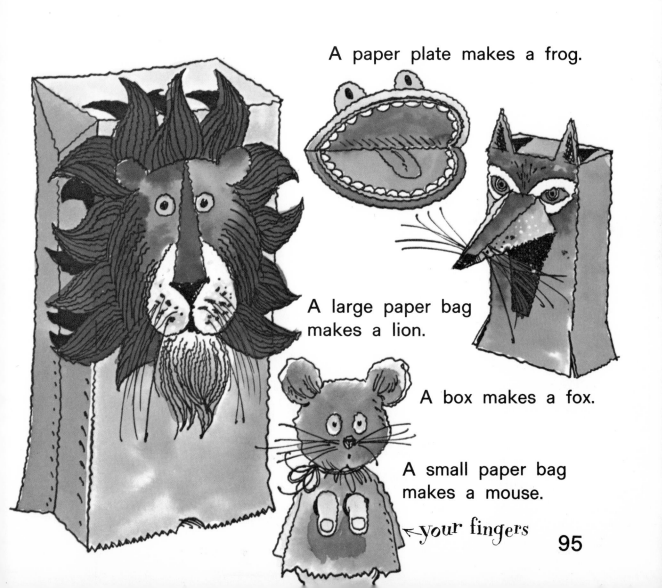

A paper plate makes a frog.

A large paper bag makes a lion.

A box makes a fox.

A small paper bag makes a mouse.

←your fingers

Dick Thompson— The Selfish Boy

Betty MacDonald

Dick Thompson was a very nice-looking boy, and he was smart in school. But whenever his name came up, people said, "Poor, poor Mrs. Thompson. She has such a problem. Whatever will she do with that boy?"

I'll bet you would feel just awful if people said a thing like that when your name came up. But Dick didn't. You see, Dick Thompson was a selfish, greedy boy. And he cared more about being a selfish, greedy boy than about what people said.

When children came over to his house to play, Dick said, "Don't touch that, that's **mine**! You can't play with that, that's **mine**! Put down **my** ball. Take off **my** hat!"

Each time his mother heard him say this, she would send him up to his room to think about how selfish he was. Dick would go right up, for he always did what his mother told him. But he didn't think about how selfish he was. He just sat on the bed and swung his legs and thought, "Everything in this room is **mine.** No one is going to touch **my** things!"

He sure was a problem.

One day Dick's mother bought
a big box of peppermint sticks.
She called Dick into the house and said,
"Now, dear, I have bought this big box
of peppermint sticks for you. But I want
you to share them with your friends.
Don't forget the little children, Dick, and
you might take one or two to the lady
next door. She loves peppermint."

Dick said, "Thank you, Mother,
for the fine candy." Then he took the box
outside and put it in the basket on the
front of his bike. He let the other
children look at his peppermint sticks.
But he told them, "This is **my** candy
and nobody can touch it!"

The children knew Dick very well. They understood that he would do something if they touched his candy. But, as they looked at the candy, they wished and wished that they could have just one stick. Dick's mother, watching from the window, saw all the children gathered around Dick. She saw the box of candy in the basket on the front of his bike.

"Just look at Dick," she thought to herself. "He's going to divide the candy with all his little friends. I just knew he would learn to share." And she waved and smiled at Dick.

Dick waved and smiled back. But just then Kim James, who wasn't afraid of anything, took a stick of candy. **CRACK!** Dick hit her on the hand.

And it was then that his mother saw what was going on. She flew out the front door, took Dick by the arm, and marched him up to his room. Then she took the box of candy and told Kim to give some to all the children.

From the window of his bedroom, Dick watched Kim divide the candy. He was very mad.

After all the candy had been divided, Mrs. Thompson went into the house and called Dick's father. She said, "Leroy, we have a problem. I'm so unhappy about Dick."

Dick's father said, "What is the matter? Is he sick?"

Dick's mother said, "No, but I wish he were. Then it would be so easy." And she told him about the peppermint sticks.

Mr. Thompson said, "Why not give him a good hard spanking? Tell him that you're going to give him something that he can keep all to himself. Ha, ha!"

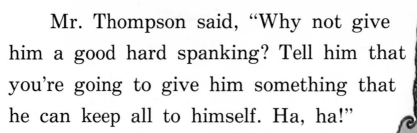

"Now, Leroy," said Mrs. Thompson. "This is not a laughing matter. I don't think a spanking will help at all. I just don't know what to do or where to turn."

Dick's father said, "I know. I know just what to do. Call that Mrs. Wiggle-Piggle or whatever her name is. You know, the one who cured Butch Brown."

"You mean Mrs. Piggle-Wiggle. Oh, Leroy, you are so wonderful! I'll call her right away," said Mrs. Thompson. She was already beginning to smile.

Mrs. Piggle-Wiggle

Mothers always do cheer up when they think of Mrs. Piggle-Wiggle because she knows so much about children. After all, she has had about nine hundred little boys and girls come to her house. They would bake cookies, play cards, have tea, and dig for gold in her back yard. She was just the one to ask about Dick, the selfish boy. And so Mrs. Thompson called her. She said, "Hello, Mrs. Piggle-Wiggle. This is Mrs. Thompson, Dick's mother."

Mrs. Piggle-Wiggle said, "Hello, Mrs. Thompson. I have been waiting for your call."

Mrs. Thompson said, "You have? Why?"

"Because I know Dick very well," said Mrs. Piggle-Wiggle. "Dick is a dear boy, but he is very selfish."

"Oh, I know he is. I know he is," said Mrs. Thompson. She was just about to cry because Mrs. Piggle-Wiggle knew how selfish Dick was.

Mrs. Piggle-Wiggle said, "Now
Mrs. Thompson, don't feel sad. Selfishness
is just like a cold. It's very easy
to cure. But we must start now,
before another day goes by. Dick is
such a nice little boy. We want
everyone to like him as we do."

"Oh, do you like him, even if he's
selfish?" asked Dick's mother.

"Yes—I do," said Mrs. Piggle-
Wiggle. "I love all children. But it makes
me sad when I see a child who has
something like selfishness, and his
father and mother don't do a thing to
cure him."

"But I want to cure Dick," said his mother. "I will do anything to cure him."

Mrs. Piggle-Wiggle said, "The Selfishness Cure is really very easy. But you must do **just** what I tell you. You will have to come down here and get my Selfishness Kit. And I will tell you how to use it."

"Thank you so much, dear Mrs. Piggle-Wiggle," said Mrs. Thompson. "I will leave right now." She put on her coat and ran all the way to Mrs. Piggle-Wiggle's house.

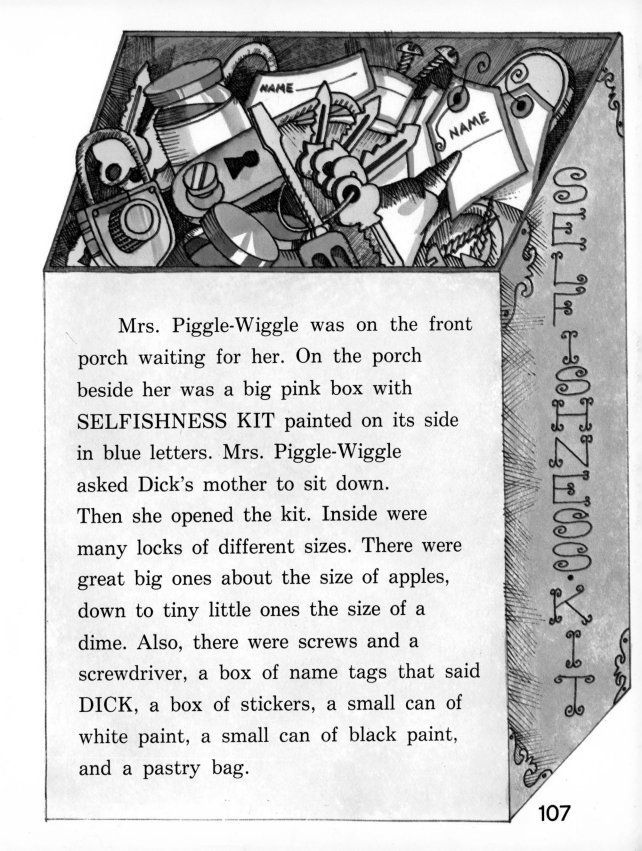

Mrs. Piggle-Wiggle was on the front porch waiting for her. On the porch beside her was a big pink box with SELFISHNESS KIT painted on its side in blue letters. Mrs. Piggle-Wiggle asked Dick's mother to sit down. Then she opened the kit. Inside were many locks of different sizes. There were great big ones about the size of apples, down to tiny little ones the size of a dime. Also, there were screws and a screwdriver, a box of name tags that said DICK, a box of stickers, a small can of white paint, a small can of black paint, and a pastry bag.

Mrs. Piggle-Wiggle said,
"Mrs. Thompson, these locks are for all
Dick's things. When you get home, put
these locks on his drawers, his bike,
his bedroom door, his toothbrush and
everything else he owns. Then give him
the keys. This is so that **he** and **he**
alone can touch his things. The name
tags are to be put on all his clothes.
And the stickers are for all his books,
his ruler, his crayons, and his paints.
On each sticker write in big letters
with this black paint DICK'S BOOK—
DON'T TOUCH! or DICK'S CRAYONS
—DON'T TOUCH!

"On every toy you must paint,
in black or white paint, DICK'S BALL—
DON'T TOUCH! or DICK'S BAT—
DON'T TOUCH! Put the name of the
toy first and then DON'T TOUCH!

"The pastry bag is to be filled
with white frosting. It is to be used
to mark Dick's sandwiches, apples,
cookies, and plate.

"That's all there is to it. I'm sure
you won't need the Selfishness Kit
for more than a week."

Mrs. Thompson said, "Are you sure
it will work?"

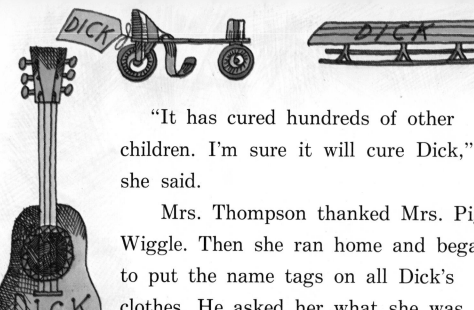

"It has cured hundreds of other children. I'm sure it will cure Dick," she said.

Mrs. Thompson thanked Mrs. Piggle-Wiggle. Then she ran home and began to put the name tags on all Dick's clothes. He asked her what she was doing. When she showed him, he was as happy as could be. "Boy, that will show people who owns my clothes," he said.

Mrs. Thompson did not say anything. She just went right on doing what she was doing. She put name tags on all Dick's clothes, even his socks. Then she opened the kit and took out a tiny lock. She locked Dick's toothbrush to the toothbrush rack. Then she gave the key to Dick. "You should find a ring to hold your keys," she said. "You're going to have a lot of them."

"Boy, that's wonderful!" Dick said, looking at the tiny key. He was thinking, "That's **my** toothbrush, and now no one but **me** can touch it." He was very happy.

When it was time for supper, Mrs. Thompson closed the Selfishness Kit and took it to show Dick's father. She told him about Mrs. Piggle-Wiggle. Mr. Thompson said he was sure everything was going to be all right.

After supper they went up to Dick's room to put on some of the locks. They were surprised to find that Dick himself had put locks on all his drawers, his toy box, and his doors. He had also put stickers on all his books, crayons, and paints. On the stickers he had printed in black paint DICK'S BOOK—DON'T TOUCH! DICK'S CRAYONS—DON'T TOUCH! DICK'S PAINTS—DON'T TOUCH! Dick was very proud. "Don't I print well?" he asked his father.

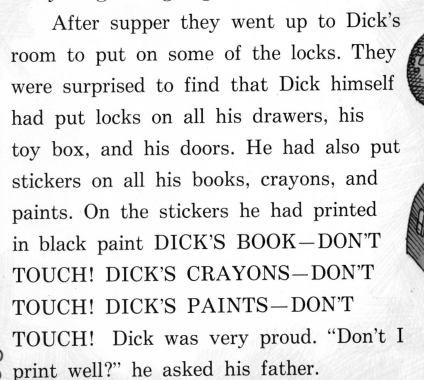

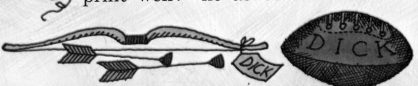

His father said, "You should be able to print well. You've had a lot of practice." And he looked sadly around the room at all the stickers.

He turned to Dick's mother and said, "Maybe we should also wear stickers. DICK'S MOTHER—DON'T TOUCH! DICK'S FATHER—DON'T TOUCH!"

Mrs. Thompson did not laugh.

Then Dick said, "Come on, let's mark all the rest of my things."

And so they worked until nine. They marked Dick's bike, his baseball, his bat, his pitcher's glove, his catcher's glove, his tool box, his lunchbox, and his toy ships. They even painted DICK'S DOG—DON'T TOUCH! on Willie's collar.

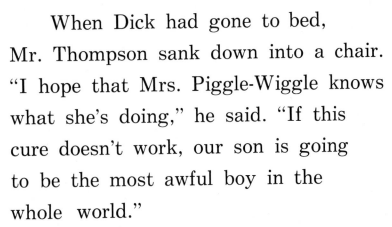

When Dick had gone to bed, Mr. Thompson sank down into a chair. "I hope that Mrs. Piggle-Wiggle knows what she's doing," he said. "If this cure doesn't work, our son is going to be the most awful boy in the whole world."

Mrs. Thompson said, "Oh, no, dear, not in the whole world!"

The Selfishness Cure

The next morning they could hear Dick working at his locks long before they were up. He was a little late coming down to breakfast because it took time to lock all his drawers and doors. But he was very happy.

While Dick was eating his breakfast, his mother packed his lunch. She marked the sandwiches, the apple, and his cookies. She marked his lunchbox, too.

After breakfast Dick put his lunchbox in his basket. He noticed the big sign on his bike. It said DICK'S BIKE—DON'T TOUCH!

At school the children didn't notice the sign on his bike. At lunch he opened his lunchbox and took out the sandwiches. They were marked DICK'S SAND-WICHES—DON'T TOUCH! The apple was marked DICK'S APPLE—DON'T TOUCH! and the cookies were marked DICK'S COOKIES—DON'T TOUCH! Everyone laughed and wanted to see them. With all the pushing, one of the sandwiches fell and was jumped on. Then some of the boys took the apple and threw it in the air. "Throw me Dick's apple," they yelled. "Oh, look, Dick's apple fell on the ground." When at last they gave Dick his apple, it was brown and soft.

That afternoon Peter Lincoln asked Dick for his ruler. When he saw the sticker that said DICK'S RULER— DON'T TOUCH! he began to laugh. He gave the ruler to Tom Howard, who laughed, too. Tom gave it to the girl in front of him. Mrs. Fisher had to come down to get it. When she saw the sign, she laughed, too. But she gave the ruler back to Dick.

DICK'S RULER-DON'T TOUCH!

After school some of the children decided to play baseball in the lot by Dick's house. Dick brought out his ball and bat, and everyone saw DICK'S BALL—DON'T TOUCH! DICK'S BAT —DON'T TOUCH! "We can't touch anything so let's go home," they said. And they went home.

Dick went up to his room to play. But he found that he had locked the key to his toy box in another box. So he went down and sat on the front porch. He listened to the children playing in Butch Brown's yard.

The next morning at school, no one would play with him. The boys and girls pointed at him, and they laughed and laughed. Mrs. Fisher came to see what the trouble was. She almost laughed herself when she saw the sign someone had put on the back of Dick's coat. It said "THIS IS DICK—DON'T TOUCH!"

At lunchtime the children gathered around to look at his sandwiches. As soon as Dick took them out, the children danced around him and sang, "Dick's sandwich—Don't touch! Dick's apple—Don't touch! Dick's lunchbox— Don't touch!"

After school Dick went right home,
but he had lost the key to his room.
So he went down to play with his
tool box. But every time he saw the big
white sign DICK'S TOOL BOX—DON'T
TOUCH! he thought of school and his
lunchbox. He thought of how the children
laughed at him. He felt just awful. At
supper his father brought him his plate
marked DICK'S DINNER—DON'T
TOUCH! Dick looked at it and said,
"Aw, why do you have to mark my plate?
I don't care which one I get."

Mrs. Thompson smiled at Mr. Thompson and said, "All right, Dick, we won't mark your plate if you will share your cake with Willie."

Dick thought for a while and then divided his cake into two parts. He gave one to Willie, who ate it down and looked happy.

After dinner Dick told his father he had lost the keys to his room. And so his father took off the locks on his doors and on the toy box. Dick said, "Don't put them back, Dad. I don't care who goes into my room or gets into my things."

MINE?

The next morning Dick got up
at six o'clock. He scraped DICK'S
LUNCHBOX—DON'T TOUCH! from his
lunchbox. He took the sign off his bike.
Then he went in to his mother. "Mom,"
he said, "please don't mark my sandwiches.
Please don't mark any of my things, Mom."

Mrs. Thompson said, "All right, Dick.
I only did it to help you."

Dick said, "I don't care who gets
my lunch. Just don't mark it."

At lunch all the children gathered
around. But his sandwiches, and his
apple, and his lunchbox were not marked.
So they ran out to see his bike. There
was no sign on it, so they sat down and
ate their lunches.

Right after school Dick ran home and scraped the marking off his bat and ball. Then he scraped the DICK'S GLOVE—DON'T TOUCH! off his glove, and walked up to where the children were playing ball. He threw the ball, bat, and glove down beside the catcher. "Do you want to use these?" he asked. "I don't care," he said, and he went back to his own house.

In a little while Kim James rang
the doorbell. She asked Mrs. Thompson
if Dick could come out and play.
Mrs. Thompson said, "He'd love to, Kim.
But first he must return something
to Mrs. Piggle-Wiggle."

Kim said, "Tell him to come over
to the lot when he gets back. And here
are some keys he lost."

SELFISHNESS
KIT

Mrs. Thompson said, "Thank you for the keys, dear. But thank goodness they are Mrs. Piggle-Wiggles's, not Dick's."

She took the keys up to Dick who was in his room. He was very busy packing Mrs. Piggle-Wiggle's Selfishness Kit.

What Someone Said When He Was Spanked On The Day Before His Birthday

Some day
I may
Pack my bag and run away.
Some day
I may.
—But not today.

Some night
I might
Slip away in the moonlight.
I might.
Some night.
—But not tonight.

Some night.
Some day.
I might.
I may.
—But right now I think I'll stay.

—*John Ciardi*

124

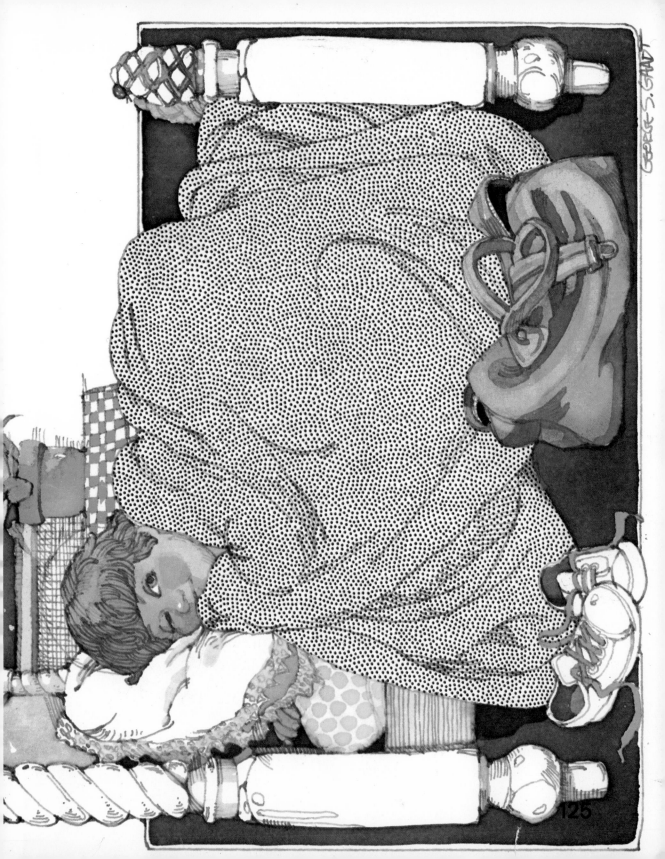

125

WORD LIST

The new words introduced in this book are listed below beside the page number on which they first appear. The children should be able to independently identify italicized words at this level.

6. mirror
   Thomas
   storekeeper
   dollars
7. puzzled
8. *carried*
   stood
   stared
   owned
   painters
   storytellers
9. *Ricky*
   Pam
10. *nights*
11. happened
    cards
    screamed
12. pitch
    plan
    office
    art
    front
    nervous
    lines
13. tiptoed
    loudly
    wake
14. *pretended*
    practiced
15. *papers*

18. *Ricky's*
    grim
    swung
    pitcher
19. *swing*
    strike
21. *sounded*
    throughout
    understood
22. *met*
    indeed
24. *Pam's*
25. *Thomas's*
28. self-portraits
    self-portrait
    picture
    artist
    pages
    artists
    mirrors
    Rockwell, Norman
30. *Dürer, Albrecht*
    Van Gogh, Vincent
    during
    lifetime
31. *Da Vinci, Leonardo*
    chalk
    age
    Johnson, Malvin Gray
    painting

32. *pictures*
    using
    corner
33. *drew*
36. *twin*
    troubles
37. cabin
    west
    beside
    stream
    fields
38. *paths*
    kept
    ducks
    babies
39. *one-room*
    schoolhouse
    grade
    seats
    spend
40. *practice*
    second-grade
    slam
    shout
    sight
41. *trouble*
    often
    trailer
    snoopers
    snoop

blackboard

43. *alike*

trip

stores

bank

since

rows

lose

45. *wall-to-wall*

46. piece

glass

48. difference

49. silver

50. *hits*

bounces

52. *lights*

54. ghost

India

barber

ghosts

barber's

Ved

cutting

men's

shaving

Ved's

left

tools

razors

brushes

combs

55. clever

I'd

rather

56. willow

fresh

57. haunted

floated

treetop

dream

dreamed

58. *quickly*

ghosts

caught

tonight

59. *course*

60. *zip*

second

bother

bought

cows

pigs

shave

61. *tricked*

63. *dared*

64. reflection

68. *five*

pod

peas

themselves

cozy

warmed

quite

pea

forever

backaches

69. *weeks*

turning

broken

which

remarkable

smallest

70. *pop*

rolling

sunshine

peashooter

71. *lazy*

board

attic

moss

hidden

forgotten

72. daughter

child

73. *taken*

root

74. *child's*

believe

shining

able

happen

thankful

tied

sill

upper

somewhere

75. *hope*

76. *hour*

bloom

leaned

kissed

77. *rooftop*

ended

round

fattest

roundest

beginning

80. *foolish*

fishermen

plays

either

82. *spots*
kneel
raft
third
lean
fourth
bridge
fifth
sixth
83. *spot*
drowned
84. *counting*
89. *points*
squeeze
90. *squeezed*
squeezes
91. *finding*
92. *bone*
carrying
greedy
other's
mouth
96. *Dick*
Thompson
selfish
nice-looking
whenever
cared
98. *Dick's*
peppermint
sticks
99. *gathered*
divide
waved
100. *afraid*
101. *marched*
bedroom

divided
102. *spanking*
ha
Wiggle-Piggle
cured
Piggle-Wiggle
103. *cheer*
nine
bake
tea
105. *selfishness*
cure
106. *kit*
107. *locks*
different
sizes
size
apples
screws
screwdriver
tags
stickers
pastry
108. *drawers*
toothbrush
owns
keys
clothes
ruler
sticker
109. frosting
mark
sandwiches
110. *thanked*
socks
lock
locked

rack
key
111. *doors*
printed
print
you've
112. *wear*
marked
pitcher's
catcher's
tool
lunchbox
ships
Willie's
113. *sank*
114. *apple*
noticed
115. *notice*
pushing
116. *Fisher*
brought
117. *Brown's*
118. aw
119. *Dad*
120. *scraped*
Mom
121. *marking*
122. *he'd*
return
123. *packing*